D0756961

Drunken
Man
On
A
Bicicyle

Drunken Man on a Bicycle

by D.S. Butterworth

LynxHousePress

Acknowledgements:

"drunken man on a bicycle," *Azure, A Journal of Literary Thought*
"Jesus Considers America," *Rock & Sling*
"deliberations of the russian king" and "the drunk on the bicycle sees his hair as a pentecostal fire" *What Rough Beast*

Printed in the United States of America.

Cover Design: Christine Holbert
Book Design: Taylor D. Waring | taylordwaring.com
Author Photo: Amy Sinisterra

FIRST EDTION

This and other award-winning titles may be viewed at www.lynxhousepress.com

Lynx House Press titles are distributed by the University of Washington Press (hfscustserv@press.jhu.edu).

ISBN: 978-0-89924-178-4

Library of Congress Cataloging-in-Publication data may be obtained from the Library of Congress.

Contents

drunken man on a bicycle

1.

A drunken man on a bicycle tumbles over streets
like a crumpled paper in the wind of history—
behold the miracle of flying trash, animal
shapes rich and strange: top hat horse head,
dinner jacket monkey, ferret and weasel
dealing five-card stud at the conference table—
marvel at the polished sheen of this inscrutable
now. Step right up: watch the raveling
of the feral woman, witness the juggling hands!
For we have decreed sacred this manner of inebriation,
this monkey riding the back of a dog godlike,
our adorations gathering as insect clouds
over the muddy waters of our borders, malarial,
heretical. Hush for the conjuring spell, marvelous
prestidigitation! For we have canonized this chaos
of handlebars, this zigzag careening through
the morning commute, this hit and run of spectators
frozen in testimony—maybe you, maybe me,
as the turning of the bicycle weaves
and veers to eat the world up.

2.

Look: the mind's windy places, secret
and wandering, fill with antic shadow,
with flotsam from underworlds of blood
and hunger, as a sham fury seizes synapse
and cell, contorts the private spaces
into marketplaces, into dread and trivial theater
drawn with chartered streets where once sang
lullabies of winter and moon, now doodled
apocalypses with clown horns and shoes.
We watch the shadows prance across a screen
and marvel as a gun becomes a magpie,
death a mouse in motley, the machine of state
a bicycle, Lord Chaos, a drunken man shape-
shifting as the wind of the mind drifts and palls.
Step right up, Ladies and Gentlemen, one and all!
We are the sad and rapturous Americans,
gunpowder connoisseurs, rubes and dupes, suckers
and sages, traitors and patriots, the enamored crowd,
brutal and incredulous, furious and mad—

3.

He rides the wind from his own mouth
as it fills invisible sails
of rumor and conspiracy,
fictive worlds blooming in his wake,
fleurs du mal, algae eating up the oxygen
in the self-same pond that is his mind—
O Kingly brain—creating one ocean
of self, receptor agonists and neurotoxins
alike declaiming verses in prophecy,
silken parachutes
of circus tents
to bless elephants and giraffes,
dressing the chimpanzees in ballroom
guise, colonizing our cerebellums,
whip, cane, scourge, and flage,
(Poor Tom's a-cold)
with cartoons of dung and arsenic.

4.

The theater loves its monkey: electric
child darting over the skull's furniture,
climbing the starlit dome, tiny proscenium,
on rumor of storm and war from the far pavilions.
Our vervet nervously picks the teeth of a baboon,
smoothes the strings of the puppet with affection.
And suddenly a new birth—Imperial Decree—
eats up our thoughts, affections, dreams, the day's
little plans and comforts, swallowed in the shadow
of billowing tent as the monkey whimpers for
the pony-riding dog, for giraffes straining
their alien faces against the radiation from facsimiles
of bellowing clowns, the famed performers, purveyors,
sleights of hand. The theater loves its monkey,
the dimensions of its secret rooms,
the music of everyday, voices from the garden,
applause for the clever quip, the committee table
triumph, the saucepan victory. But read in the eyes
the fixed attention, imagining the rousted salute,
the cartoon report drawn in blood, artillery echoing
through the hills of the approaching weather.
November is the cruelest month: Run Monkey, Hide!
The lever you pressed for candy now delivers shock,
but you keep pressing to burn, to weep and burn and mock.

5.

The man on the bicycle believes he is America.
He rides the cities and plains, intoxicated.
Maybe like me, maybe like you,
he climbs the ladder of weeks, a clown
on a wind-up scooter with a wheel that limps.
He imagines he is hauling bones of enemies,
but they are the ribs and femurs of a king in a sack,
but they are heavy and wheeze as he rides,
but the sack is his body and the bones are his own,
but he steers toward a shiny bauble at the curb,
a silver rattle he can shake to remind
himself that he is king and scepter of the world.

6.

A tide of faces rises on his screen, a field
in spring after rains, before drought. The child
he carries inside climbs his ribs astonished
that so many have traveled to Earth from
whatever stars to peer out of these hollow
eyes of oxidized bronze. Bells ring down
the beginnings and the endings as time
rages above the faces in tongues of flame.
He surveys tombs of men who ruled and died,
of women who ruled and died, of painters
who rendered the gestures and motions as women
and men: naked or nun, impresario or clown.
Maybe he's them, maybe he's us. Maybe this
is metaphysical theater he mistakes for simple
circus, Punch and Judy, the awkward puppets
splayed beneath loosened strings, where
he points to the fire-eater, the contortionist,
illusionist and knife-thrower—and we ask, Daddy
what are those men doing behind that curtain?
He says: don't you want to see the naked lady too?

7.

The child inside him squeezes the man's heart
in his hands to drain the darkness. *Where greatness?*
he asks and scans *TV Guide*. Now the child covers
the bicyclist's eyes from behind and the whole
balancing act teeters, a stone street trapeze,
Tiresias's eyes blinded by a naked Venus of himself,
as if careening through this flood of faces he might
extinguish the image. But no, pyrotechnics flare,
the child's hands a miracle of loaves and fishes
scattering across mall and piazza, the crowd's accordion
dilations like birds flocking in wind over the river
to avoid the magic bicycle as it casts spells
and curses, a hanged man rattling in the spokes.
The drunkard rolls beyond control through
an old banker's heart, through pockets of merchants,
ledger books of bloodwork paid in gold and silver.
He fishtails through sodden plaster, through crowds
of pilgrims along the muddy river and over
the stones that are the body of civilization as it sleeps.
He wobbles like an Etruscan, almost driving
into their same dark soil with their words and gods
a cumulous contrail behind his metal horse.
Besotted with his sole self image naked and devouring,
his great star rises and sets beyond wisps of hair-like cloud.

8.

The drunk on the bicycle is America and its king,
is the crowd and ghost of crowd, he is the sleeping
part of the mind, the ranges where geometrical
shapes of urge and fallacy swim in amniotic darkness,
Babylons of desire, Jerusalems of memory,
the lace and stone corners where birds and apes
have gone haywire in imagination's mausoleum.
The bicycle steers its own course through a hall
of mirrors where etched script traces stories
of the plagues—here a map scorned face and tribe,
there stands a man in tin where the blood and flesh
wrung out long ago, here demons wore a path
over mountains, there demons mowed the villages,
as if to say these are the yourselves you used
to be, you walk the streets to dream and sing
in the emptiness: *me my little self am this I*
an animal singing in the new world's reliquary.
The bicycle weaves through a Gettysburg
of becoming and dreams itself as the only tin, the only
aluminum facsimile of candleflame in the damp cellar
of dark-swallowing light reborn as acetylene torch.

9.

A clown on a bike! We laugh, we cringe, we cry,
what can go wrong, we wonder, moments before we die.
His elliptical motions a delirium, his huffing
breath a spawn of words as cartoon monsters,
squadrons of machines, bristling with missiles,
famine and war bursting like thought bubbles
from the burlesque of a body as it weaves. We thrill
at the force of the man as a bicycle morphs
into tank and turret—but is it in a dream he flicks
battalions from his shoulder with a sneeze? We
only see the syphilitic jester, the chimpanzee
bullying his way to the front of the line with daddy's
swag, for the imponderables of the child
in the control room configuring himself as a man
who scratches an itch at his back with whole economies,
sneering at entire cities as if they were mosquitoes,
knocking over forests like Alamos in a game of skittles,
as the horror drowns into a whimper. The bicycle
of the imagination steers like a fish in air,
unstable, insecure, a wavering gaze,
a stumbling clutch of smoke, inebriate, debauched,
surfing on the contempt pumping through his own heart
so full of gasoline it blinds him to the pure sway
of stasis, to the still point he might find and hold,
and delivers him into the inertia of asteroids in orbit.
Maybe you laugh, maybe you cry, maybe you sleep
and dream: no body forgets how to ride a bike,
the taste of candy, the thrill of circus tents billowing
in the wind of childhood—Mommy, why is the Ringmaster
grabbing the trapeze lady, why is he falling down?

10.

And now all the mad people are speaking into their hands:
Behold the colored whirligigs above the Congress,
the painted horses galloping in a ring!—here
a Bush stepped on a stone, there a Kennedy
combed her hair, look at the way that façade shapes
the sky, how the dome becomes massive against
the storm of change. Now the crowd raise their hands
to prove they were here before the world was free,
and now they turn their hands to carving
a nation into sunlit chiffons, now they wrestle demons
into the earth, death by drowning, death by arrow,
death by sword, death by edict, death by directive,
death by mercury and arsenic, death by demon air—
beautiful death by ink sluiced off newspapers
into tinctures of anger and confusion, death to all
but the immaculate self, tax-less and finally free—
what a show. The biggest crowd ever.
Voices rise to hail the invention of a new
mathematics, new words blare like bassoons
and charters and decrees to spin it all up
in a giant cocoon so they can give birth
to freedom as dark matter, ink the intoxicant
free from words, free from meaning, free
from anarchist's slogans, free like machines
with wings, like monkeys with leathern wings
chattering across a cobalt sky. The drunken man
on the bicycle follows his wheels where they
lay tracks of a new language weaving through mud,
a new tongue twisted into dark screens
as a Babel of people speak into their palms

where ghosts have gathered according to the spell:
O let us drink the moon and light our way
with candles and follow a trail of wax
as the wheeled contraption cranks
the drunken man home—all ye all ye home come free.

11.

A Napoleon in motley, a Medici in rags,
a Machiavelli of the people. His wheel razes
crooked roadwork stones—let us number them
so we can re-assemble the puzzle the way some
Khrushchev or Goebbels, some Stalin or Mao
will recognize as history's inevitability. Let us dream
some deep chemical architecture of a new nation
to fresco over the ashes of memory. Pace the towers
of the Khan, O Senator, prowl the towers of the inebriate
King, O Congressman, pace the broken crenellations
and scout for rumor from seas, pace the battlements
beyond the rising rivers, beyond waters pressing the wall,
cheer the siege with saltless foes, grind the enemy's
palaces to dust, destroy the narcotic televisions,
burn the veils of silk, strafe the caravans and turn the sand
to glass. Read the flight of crow, the fire's ash, augury
of tea leaves in the cup, prophesize gold in futures
of arsenic and polonium. Trade alphabets like pilgrims,
cast the Phoenicians and Greeks into a copper pit,
bargain for astrolabes to navigate the bays, climb
the profit sheets on a ladder of ribs cured
from the carcasses of your slaves, piss on the agonies
of the old wars the piss of vodka and gasoline,
hammer failed hope into a facsimile of a horse
in tin and ship it to an antique market, stamp a dull dollar,
florin, or ruble and awaken the muddy river of your America.
Rise again like matin bells flaring over the rooftops and sing
our past to parchment, powder the eggshells, spit on the coffins,
eat breadcrumb and marrow and declare your nation in Cyrillic.

Follow the dopplering of the motorcade, trace the path
of your soused shadow toward an uncertain star
in the middle distance that burns through sleep
against a terracotta dome, against a tower some Cosimo
watches anxiously to execute the hour's newly minted curse.

﹡

12.

If there's a form inside a thing, like a human
shape inside a rock, then there's a miracle
of balance inside a drunk on a bicycle
navigating the streets of the brain—
maybe he just cannot lose. Congressmen
leech mutability like phosphorous
into the flickering crowd
almost knocking the king from his seat
atop a contraption of wire and steel
some fool sketched in a notebook
so this huffing dervish could go forth
to raise his flag of money
where the pandemonium of history
refuses to die on a chalk-silhouette street.
We are composed of newspaper, rag, cigarette butts,
emulsifiers, wool, and a gold florin.
Some prince's man watched a drunkard
on a horse once and invented the cantilevered
arm. That is how we abandon nature for art—
not to praise some god who remains aloof,
but to hail the King, to worship the thing burning
inside him like Dionysius' ruby bead: our crimson flail.

13.

Grief brings the minstrel to the old city
where corporate towers were built in stone
that only dreamed of plastic and strontium,
where the first corporate engines ate a fuel
of dye and blood and minted nickel reveries—
O lost home between fields and citadel,
O fatal renaissance, fevered dream,
O pool of demons who rise and flood furies
through my mind to drown the child inside,
some poor Lorenzo or Lincoln swept up
by memory's distortion of time's waters,
some Roosevelt a duke smiled to scorn
while still holding my slender slats of rib
to peer out at his future: a crowd
weighed down with purses and bags who step
on stilts like herons poised to stab at minnows.
I cycle against the tide, the throng, the groundlings
under the loggia. I ride through all these selves
staring into their hands as they go.
I sing and try to rise above the swirling radionuclides
but falling fail, drown and drop, orphean.
The underworld has many windows
open to the narcotic of widowed night.
The present moment is an ancient place.
It rises in towers above our towns,
above this you, above this me, above the shore
where Pluto fills his digital well to baffle
a revenant . . . . even a drunkard knows the length
of his hand. We ride somnambulant, a trinket
on a mobile's scale, a clown rowing a Napoleon

hat through a madman's blueprint of the near future
or recent past, a balancing suspense that cannot last
like wind from the east, as if time had seen its ghost.
Poor Tom. Peace, Smulkin. The violets wither.

14.

Witness: when the drunken man rides his bicycle
through the piazza, we recoil and advance
like mice at the mercy of his whims: now he bumps
the fruit vendor, now he glances off the window
at the bank, now he knocks over the woman
with sacks of groceries—passersby catch the oranges
and apples and bottles but the drunkard lifts
his hand in triumph: what dexterity, what balance,
what a man! A taxi smashes into the pharmacy
to avoid the wheeling bike, the man on the church
steps flinches as more broadcast groceries arc
toward him in a trajectory of circus colors.
The scene unfolds with logic and necessity,
and however reluctant we may be
to devote ourselves to him, a part of us gives it up
for the randomness of what he'll do next,
for the careening of the wheels, for the tossed
curse and catcalls as he lifts his legs
into the shape of a nun's wimple athwart the frame,
balance askew, final catastrophe now certain.
And it is like both the strophe and antistrophe
of old tragedy and the child whose antics
dominate the room. Caution and concern
become the edge of their own cutting blade
as a virtual somersault, like the inebriate tumbling
over cartoon cobblestones in a cartoon fit,
spills pedestrian blood like graffiti against the walls.

15.

On the stage it's a monkey riding a bicycle,
but in the world beyond the mind, balloons
are bombs, antics and hijinks are carnage
and war, feint and bluff are rebar
and white hoods. On the stage the tyrant is a toy,
in the world, murder. A simple sneer
and a whole people maligned, a gesture
of self-promotion, sleeves shot at the expense
of an entire race, a swerve, a honking of the toy
horn, a clown flares smilingly, the monkey primping,
stoking the furnace of self idolatry, stroking the tiny
member with a grin. Too, the nation's monkey
mind, barbarous and trivial, flickers
in the imagination of continents, a smirk flashes
over the mirrors of self and the illusions multiply
in the lurid light of the baboons' crimson asses' glow.
The audience is gullible, sincere, naïve, trembling,
half in love with the wag. Then the network spills
its headline: Jesus must have been a hater too, love
his lash and whip. Blessed are the righteous,
for they will vanquish the losers. We retreat
to the altar of television and screen, for sex
and bedtime stories in thrall of the monkey
and his coined wilderness. See the cigarette
in the adorable grip of the baby chimp, see
a thousand fires smoldering in the nation's upholstery.
Each crimson coal bores a hole through eternity
to the underworld of dreams, anorectic
and chemical, drowned in the pupil-blackened
hatches tattooed against the believers' scored palms.
Violent night, holy night.

16.

Surely we've come to the end of something,
the end of the same thing we thought we saw die
when B-52s climbed the whirligigs of jungle
trees and shut their eyes against the napalm,
when drenched sands redeployed the groans
with pit-bulls and the hard-wired genitals
of the enemy were renditioned in old palace walls.
Were we bankrupt all along, those false hopes
we called enlightenment and renaissance
dying all these years from heartworm wheedling
doubt into sawdust however much we wished
to have, along the battlements, the muffled darkness
unfold to reveal some origin or answer, either right
or wrong? Surely we have travelled here
to see some tangle of hope and despair loosened
at a border crossing under shade of a mesquite,
only to find a wounded king fishing in the mud,
a sick queen disguised as a beggar to undo
desire or desire's obliteration—surely we have
travelled here to find something that will make us
feel whole again, or purposefully broken,
a code switch obscure scribes predicted
on a master stone a dead age scored and read
eons ago that will make us say this is our *us*:
this is what and what for, this the room,
this the bed, this the door that leads to a door,
this the word that found a home on our tongue
before it died in our ears, before it turned to ash,
this the gorgon face tattooed on the wall
of an inconsequential heart. And now a monkey

riding a scooter on a horse's back—maybe it's you,
maybe it's me who wears an impresario's top hat,
ringmaster whip in hand to beat down the humanity.
Sleep, Nuncle, sleep. Poor Tom will make him
weep and wail, his horn is dry. They will lay him
in the cold ground, at his heels a stone.
Pansies for thoughts.

17.

A clown serving plums to a voracious queen:
we know enough to know this is how it begins,
crumbs of words sprinkled across the dark
pool that opens inside an ego's screen. Furies
clamber up ribs, their faces surfacing like fish
taking shapes of desire that never died. And now
they morph and molt, swell and worm,
shed and ming from the atoms of the broken
centuries. This is what the old debris do
in fertile earth: seek and find their way to light,
the tubers half rotten, half green with rot,
ancient hatreds, buried jealousies. The end of peace
begins with war, roots of blood stirring
in new dirt. A monstrous imagination
gestates, disseminates fire and blood,
seeks purchase in the soil of the angry class.
Must all the monsters we slay wear our own faces?
(The child within slew me with just this sword
to cut the old man's ravings: rosemary, rue).

18.

We need a Medusa at this end of things,
a head of hair composed of snakes.
We need to cut out a heart and eat it
in the marketplace of this America,
we need to hold up Perseus' head
as the emblem of the new gorgon
the colonizer of minds, weaver of illusions—
O Child: decipher the aged stains
we read as prophecy growing up
from age's dregs in childhood's cup.

19.

America grows old. Mesmerized, scripted
on a screen, we watch the man on the bicycle
careen in antic shapes of a clown, a wind-up
toy or grainy cartoon with a wobbly music
of Betty-Boop or Popeye, saint or Madonna
in a black and white film or school-kid doodles
in a tablet turned flip-book—look at the man
who holds his brain like a flute of rare vintage
precarious over the cobblestones, look at his dog,
Little John, race ahead in a dream of rut
through the ancient arcades.
Look at the pantomime desire apes
aping desire, a monkey on a tin horse,
calavera on a cattail reed:
Step up right this way!—watch a man
turn into a spume of dust, watch a nation
crumble into a spatter of zinc and neurotoxins.
Behold the drunken man on the bicycle
veering over the flagstones of history,
smashing monuments like stale cookies
groping the perfumed bodies pressed
against a wall. . . . listen to the laughter
of the crowd . . . . there's a mouth on a drunken
bicycle floating on a blue ocean,
a voice whose wheels ride on currents
from his own lungs, the thermals his voice
amplifies in his cave and in the world
rising now as, airborne, he teeters toward
you and toward me, toward the opiate
oblivion of a trinket vendor's stall.

20.

Our faces are trinkets in a vendor's stall,
ears are nests a crow's lust for glitter
has feathered with silver.
The King colonizes the weak places.
A fontanel erodes under weather
of a radio voice. A god worms
the apple where the vulnerable
flesh of fruit has built its private
sweetness. The whine of a blood angel
tells history how it must unfold,
how flesh will become juice,
how the self will be deployed
in wars as the host cheers for madness,
as the nation thrills to be a toy
in the hands of a drunken man,
a bauble to juggle, words as toys
in the teeth of the drunken man,
whose medieval locomotions assemble
civic order of catapult and wagon.
Not me, not you, but hailed
as the only purity,
the one wild card,
infused with his own blood,
flush with chemicals and courage.
America, the original word,
the only beginning,
the only brave word.

21.

Hog in sloth,
fox in stealth,
dog in madness.
Come, unbutton here.
Maybe it was only
a small coin,
to have been so easily
given away,
our America.
We must wear
our rue
with a difference,
savor
the world's eating.

22.

Somewhere beyond the reach
of nation we remember voices
outside the window
beyond the hedge,
maybe you, maybe me,
sunlight and headlights
shifting across a wall,
plastic men in cinderblock
puddles, all bright as colors:
cars, flavors, sounds.
Somewhere beyond
the reach of nation you and I
remember the animal
building its nest in the shadow
of a well where
a traveler stops for water.
Somewhere beyond
the wrenching
and the howls,
drink, Traveler,
and be confused again.

23.

A canvas tent folds into steel and air
and Monkey sleeps on the neck
of a horse. Baboon murmurs
against the solar plexus
of the contortionist.
The world fills with smoke
and lavender.
Pilgrims begin a road
paralytics and lepers limped
in darkness.
The kilns forge gorgon masks.
Fragments. Sparks.
Houses of paper shift in wind.

the return of the king

In the long afternoon an angel with a sword
slept in the fireplace as the world rained.
The news report wasn't an insanity
and it wasn't a circus.
It was the return of the king.
The battlements were made
of paper no one would read.
And lamentations of the Queen.
It wasn't symbolism.
It wasn't prophecy.
It was hunger.
A new, willful appetite
raveled up in the eye of a raptor.
The king, unassailable, rolled his pink limbs
across the pixels of their screens.
The angel awoke and read old news
in the business section of the morning paper,
invested heavily in pork bellies and stars,
gold and carbon. The world continued
to rain. The years vanished into the accordion
folds of the millennia. Birds passed by
overhead, feeders in the yards
swaying in wind.

deliberations of the russian king

We need a Siberia. We need a purer
bloodstream of oil and vodka—we need
a new cocktail: nine parts vodka
one part gasoline. We're all dying anyway,
we only need to admit it.
Like poorly mixed paper-mache,
the powdered clay keeps falling from us.
(Soon I'll be a real boy.)
Isn't it the Cossacks play polo
with the carcass of a goat
or the heads of their enemies?
We need more of that.
Or were they immigrants?
Was it czars or Arabs wore
those flattened red party hats?
What we need about Russia
is the vastness. It suits us. Don't they
call prairies *steppes* over there? We
can see Doctor Zhivago climbing
all the way to heaven after his gumar,
what's her name, yeah—Lara,
in a blaze of balalaikas. That's
another thing we need. Wasn't it
Genghis Khan whose DNA is in 25%
of humanity? What's not to like?
That's a lot of matryoshka dolls.
We think of our daughter.
Hot matryoshka dolls.

royal decree

The drunk on the bicycle
tests the air not for rumor
of spring's chaos of blos-
soms or the sky's riot with
an approaching storm, not
for the mood of the city,
or even to measure the car-
bon quotient of his words
as echoes of his edicts spi-
raling out, spending them-
selves as noise alongside
the highway corridors. No,
he's sensing the space that
remains for him to occupy:
rooftops' lovely surfaces
alien and menacing, open
to a blue of endless possi-
bility. He'll have to fix that.

the drunk on the bicycle performs royal
   contemplations

There's a drunk riding a bicycle through the streets
of America who wonders why they don't get out

of his way when they see his crown. He has decreed
the end of weather, but cowers against the growing

storm. The hot wife in the sidecar is under contract
to agree, but not to touch the swollen fingers

or to be touched by their pink flanges; she has seen
a baboon in trousers work as a ventriloquist's dummy,

and understands there are languages she doesn't
wish to know how to speak. As she vanishes, the bicycle

tilts against reason like a whirligig in a gust of wind,
like the swirls the drunkard got at the inauguration, his wheels

ripping free of the weight of history like the tiny
umbrellas they place in those daisy drinks, or those stiff

skirts ballerinas wear, hair plastered like taffy tiaras
across their delicate heads, thin as bird shell. Which

makes him think again of a Russian king needing
a Russian queen, or how he'll banish the little nations

huddled around the mother country like chickadees
around the hen—and now it's as if he has awakened

and it has stopped snowing, but he is in a muddy ditch
with darkness wearing a harness of stars. Thank god he'd worn

clean underwear like his mother told him—what if the Gestapo
had found him, or the social services of his enemies,

and thank god he's germ-a-phobic, thank god nature abhors a
    vacuum—
for he's got a bicycle to ride, and a crown that glitters as he goes.

on the wings of the contraption

The wings are made of skin
patched and sewn in scale patterns
that continue to swarm as they move.
A child brushed against them
once when the drunk veered
onto the sidewalk near the shoe
fixery. She found the leathery surface
full of gaps and fetid spans
that ate the child up as he passed.
We die from the outside in.
The digested child slipped through
an intestine of keys, drivers' licenses,
a million coins, a billion bullets,
a chaos of stars and ribbons
until she caught her finger
in gears of petrified wood
that cranked those wings
into the motion a bicycle makes
under the direction of a drunken
man gesturing toward the wall
of the detention center.
These are the metaphysics.
Her blood drained
like cars emptying the suburbs,
like cattle crossing a border,
the way a nation dies,
from the inside out.

america is a paper house

The paper house burns a digital smoke,
numbers infinitesimal as drops of rain,
particles of water in a fine fog, motes
in a dust storm swimming against
the neighborhoods, burning.
The paper house is covered
in an ink of petrochemicals,
the paper walls are saturated skin,
wrinkled and swollen.
The drunken man on the bicycle
folds the paper of the nation
into a party hat. Into an airplane.
Into aborted origami swans
he sets alight
to watch the smoke
rise along the downstream
as we die.

royal decree: twelves

Because we're bigger and better, the biggest and best,
we decree we will now have twelve fingers, apostles—
our twelve Arthurian knights, though we don't believe
in fairytales, but we will believe in our twelve,
the mighty, like the zodiac signs we think,
like the days of Christmas, because we do like
glitter and glass balls, the largest number named
in a single-syllable: maybe we'll work on that
too, duo-decade, duodecal— didn't Hercules perform
twelve labors? There was a beautiful beautiful man,
we loved him, Hercules, we loved him.
Maybe if we were to repeat things twelve times
we would ascend bodily into the heaven we don't
really believe in, because if it existed, how could
it compare with our earthly towers? There's a name
for this idea, and it happens twelve days afterwards
—epiphany, a digit for every month.
Twelve Angry Men—now there was a movie,
there was a movie. Oops—is that the aura of thermal-
nuclear blast? What is this grit in our teeth?
Not to worry, it's beautiful. Things may be ugly for a while,
but then we'll wipe out war from the face of the earth,
with our twelves, our ambassadors, our golden spokes,
our missiles, our dicks. Ah crap, didn't that Boleyn
bitch have extra fingers, wasn't that a sign that she was
a sorceress?—God, remember that pig with the gloves
in the pageant last year, but hey, weren't kings born
to solve such problems? Hank the Eighth: there was a king,
marital policy to die for . . . . The picture

of our enemies' heads on stakes stirs like sildenafil
and births a new idea: maybe there's room
for a thirteenth month in our name, and thirteen—
because everything is better bigger,
because thirteen is even bigger than twelve . . . .

the drunk on the bicycle sees his hair as a pentecostal fire

Wind is life, and a moving bicycle manufactures a wind
that violates the principles of hair when the rules

of order operate according to vanity. A nun's
wimple would work the prow of his face toward

the eternal beachhead that is the world. But he hates
nuns. His eyes, too, squint from blanched lids at the grit

that makes him want to banish the silicates always crumbling
at the seams of infrastructure. It may be shellac

breaking down in his self-generated gust, or treason
of the tire tread funneling up microscopic debris

into the slipstream of irritation before his face.
He composes a law even as the sound of his breath

swims to him through the fog of exertion and the fact
of his labor. Work is for the plebes. Lord of the machine,

he considers abolishing existence—why a bicycle,
why a street, why legs and pumping heart, at all?

He grimaces as if a vision were to emerge from his bowels.
Where was he going? What was it he needed to tweet,

that joke about Dopey fucking penguins? He laughs and feels
a moment of joy, the intoxication of movement, of telling

the wheels where to go, having them comply. And when
he sees his reflection in the window he knows he has been

touched by the finger of the gods, his hair swelling bigly,
report of his enemies' immolation redolent in a tongue of flame.

white russian

The Russian King tells his America
never mind; he dreams of his daughter;

he wants to sprinkle polonium over the heads
of scientists; he wants the faces around him

to be prettier so he can use the word *gorgeous*
more often; he wants a winter cast on the skin

of his subjects to cancel out tones of dusk,
those millions of twilit frauds he will send south

where that giant sucking sound will make them
someone else's problem; he wants to paint

the insides of his tanning booth eye cups
Siberian white like the eyes of those weird

huskies, wolves maybe; he wants white
to matter again like it did when Ahab

discerned in it a god he sailed the seven
seas to worship; sometimes you must kill

the thing you love to make room for your
idea of it, so you can polish it into a rare

sapphire where you can still see, if you really
look, a glimmer of even older ideas like

freedom or justice from behind the glass,
between the bars. Such beautiful dreams. Meh.

string theory

There's a dog inside the monkey inside the puppet,
strings tied to that dinner table where pride and shame
turned forks and spoons toward the furnaces
beyond their mouths, strings tied to windy
afternoons when expectations dwindled
in the melting gaze of the father's grave
imperiousness. The dog hauls in the bones,
cowers anticipating lashes. The monkey is the one
who twitches at rules stamped on the body of the dog,
shrinks when the voices in the room go away
and he is left to his own impulses and the hungers
of the dog. The monkey's ventriloquisms
have carried him far, all the way to these pavilions
and the masticating crowds. There are multitudes
inside as well who, by some strange metallurgy, surface
at rallies with baskets of phrase and spleen, where rage
and contempt magically breed to nourish the starved
yet fruited plains of the nation. Particle and wave
become indistinguishable from one another
when we twist enough strands together. The puppet's
straw head bobs as the monkey leaps from bale to bale,
something fundamental gone haywire, something grown
so loose it is hard to believe it ever held together.
And now dog and monkey and puppet talk into tin
cans connected by cotton string. They mistake each
other's voices for distant artillery, for television

from another room, for the whine of a drone
sweeping low over the compound, for the dog's
foot scratching as it moves in dream, for
the hush of wind over the widening desert.

what we said about the stone

We said the stone must only speak stone.
We said the stone warmed as we held it
in our hands. We drilled a hole in the stone
and it didn't tremble. The stone floated on
the ocean. We said the stone was an orphan
child. We said we wanted to sell the stone.
We tried to eat the stone. We said after being
touched it stopped being the stone. We said
it wasn't the right kind of stone. We said at all
costs we must keep the stone from other stones.
We said we must keep the stone pure.
We said the blood would never wash clean.
We said everything you say about the stone
is false. We measured it and weighed it.
We sang of its blue specks and deep gray
atmosphere. We traced the history of the stone.
We put hair on the stone. We wrote the laws
of the stone on the stone. We polished the stone.
We threw the stone at a child.
We forgot about the stone and then we found
the stone again. We forbade the handling
of the stone. We said it was an Arctic stone.
We said it was made of radioactive dust
from Sirius. We said it formed when magma
heated sedimentary layers beneath the Tigris-
Euphrates. We said it didn't matter. We went
to war for the stone. We said it was all
that mattered. We said the stone was from God
and bled when we were wounded, wept when we fell.

We said it was evil. We said it was the softest
substance on the planet. We said it was as hard
as law. We said it was an egg. We said it was
a gun. We said it was a covenant. We said
it was our father. We saw the stone in a burning
bush. We said the stone rained from heaven.
We said the stone was our mother. We placed
the stone in a glass case. We placed the stone
in the ocean. We split the atoms of the stone.
We grew the stone into flowers. We said
the stone is a woman. We said it is a man.
We said the stone is the word of God.
We said we must cover its face. We said
it is the bone of a horse that ate the grain
of Nineveh. We said the stone set sail from Cork.
We said the stone is a saint. We looked inside
the stone and saw the galaxy. We looked
inside the stone and saw Satan. We looked
inside the stone and saw our own faces.
We said the stone is a lie. We said the stone
is the only truth. We said the mountain will
come to the stone. We said the stone
is from the wall of a well in Jerusalem.
We said the stone was no longer stone.
We said the stone came from Stalingrad.
We said foreigners are stealing the stone.
We said the stone is our mystery. We said
the stone is our only fact. We said we must
know the stone, worship it. We said we
must bury the stone or lose it forever.
We said the stone is a tomb. We said
the stone is a door. We said the stone

is a word. We said we will always have
the stone now, it is part of us, unredeemable,
irrevocable, cancelled, burning, indelible,
perished, permanent, void.

molecular

We wish to wash in the carbons
of the mine tailings, in the arsenics,

in the juice of papaya irrigating
the chameleons lazing in the republic of our

mind. Maybe this means Florida,
the citrus carotenes of the gulfstream

clambering up the ribs of the towers
like wee chimpanzees. Scenery is a mental

trick we've learned to cultivate as day
dream between phases of the moon,

or during repetition of words as we
give a speech. We like the way

the drift's *tabula rasa* leads
to the anarchy emerging

from our mouth: sudsy waters,
a blue turban in flame, veined lizards,

a boiled egg, textile factories, carburetors
clogged with flat, stale sulfides, synapses

deranged with pharmaceutical possibility.
We survey our dominions and conclude

it's time for a good lie about the Pope.
A battalion of hats from a noisy arena

push us halfway to a recognition of where
we are, what we were about to say.

Somewhere inside we pull a lever
on the Laz-E-Boy and put our feet up,

the ponderous shoes sometimes heavy,
but now light as colored balloons,

and let the mouth do the work
even as we come to something like

a realization that the new economy will
hinge on the physics of extraction,

on drills puncturing abscesses just below
the brain of the continent to open up the rot

and stink and haul it out with anti-bacterials
slaving away like microscopic dwarves

with microscopic shovels and picks,
in that in-between where all the little people

dwell, in that grey space they call a nation
halfway from stellar to molecular.

the king under siege

Why are dogs upset that he said he was a cat person,
why the cats upset he said he was a dog?
Covering all the bases in gold leaf was never easy,
but it's the kind of clown he is to please them all.
Where can he find a bottle of sober in this place,
and where can he get laid—the stiff wheel of his collar
is getting in the way, and all the taffeta and crinoline
strain the kind of cool he is when he is putting on
the moves. What they say about clowns and tears
really is true. Even the commies hated the wicked
witch, so what's the big deal? So true. He hoped
the gummy bears would help him skewer the pale queen
at countless rallies, and now all the committees are
trying to prove that he meant it? At times like these
he wishes he had a horse, that he looked better half-
naked bareback, a force to be reckoned with, or yet,
even better, one of those half-horse half-man thingies
that would get the ladies' attention. A flat tire is
his sad tragedy, and when he bends down to look,
the world swirls. Never has a drunk on a bike
been treated so poorly by the people. It must be his
precious enemies again: who doesn't love a bike
on a high wire? So what if it's only a street.
Who could hate a circus? Even if it is only finger puppets.
What he needs is bright lights and a really
loud bang to thrill his people—there are enough
fay little high-heeled bastards need blowing away.
Besides, the people put him on this bike. Some-
thing is happening under the cone of his hat, as if
one or two of the bells have loosened and are rattling

across the taut skin of his crown, crumbs sprinkled
on a goldfish bowl and now, swimming up from depths
like an amphibious jack boot from primordial slime,
opening its eyes and mouth to prophesize war:
the popsicle and bourbon, the testosterone and steel,
the thistle and adrenaline balloon of a single hatchling thought.

heartland

Mites wheedle at bones of the nation,
at marrow of a skyline rectilinear
with opioid derangements.
We wander gravel roads
waiting to become fossils
brewing the future's fuels.
Our nursed grievances hatch
reptile bodies to eat the roots
where they are most tender,
against morning light's
methamphetamine cast.
Our new colons stomach new needs:
anger is the hunger of the hour
and vestigial organs awaken
to grind its calciums.
The era of the possible
fills with caffeine and Ritalin
as we baptize our children
brought forth in sorrow.
From the corporate fields
animal fats swell up like music
irrigated by pharmaceutical dreams
bringing a greatness back
to amber waves of grain
in the arteries of the heartland.

america: a disphoria

In this unending circus the tents never close.
In this fever of the mind the Impresario drones
through the halls of the weary imagination
and at the edge of sleep a Halloween of shapes
shadows out: the dog-faced boy and gap-toothed
crone hovering like harpies as even the splendid
autumn afternoon echoes with the galloping of blue
ponies. Sequins fall from the tights of the trapeze
starlet and always the whip crack of the lion
tamer reports like cries from all those guns
keeping us free. The voice barks and fills the dome
of bone, and the mind of the nation bleeds again,
breathes the circus that now burns through ages.
Armies deploy their petroleum distillates
at the rumor of peasants, gather from Kevlar baskets
miracles of lead and mercury against the children.
Smoke lingers above the gated communities
to anthems swelling from pipe organs. A chimpanzee
peels off his hide to become a lion, the lion peels
off its hide to become a giraffe, a flamingo,
mouse, horse, otter, bear, and poof—
it's the master of ceremonies, Impresario.
Ringmaster barks partisan prestidigitations,
cries the cartoon marvels morphing
through the hippodrome. Torch-juggling
acrobats muster to answer the idea of a menagerie
winding toward the border, their zebras and camels
mumbling incantations to soothe the militias.
The patriots clap, the patriots roar, the patriots
wheel out the mighty human cannonball

that launches into pure air and unfolds
into the mighty shape of a clown riding a bicycle
in only air all the while the banks convulsing
in an ecstasy of fox fur and feathers nestling
the derivatives and their new instruments.
Everyone loves the circus: we laugh, we cry,
we watch the Ringmaster move his mouth.
Utterances become nature, women solidify
into ancient forms as the battle between word
and body ends with a decree: High and Mighty,
I am delivered naked unto your empty lots.
And now a parade of archetypes assembles
to hammer down the open door of the tent
(Impresario plays solitaire behind the flap
so bored with the discovery of opposable thumb).
Children must be born to fill the cannons with their
perfect shapes and the fragrance of quince
from their heads. We are swept away
by voices as a trapeze army enters town:
magician and hooper, knife-thrower and clown.
We eat our god, we shoulder our guns,
we rage, salute, and genuflect, to prepare
ourselves for the sacrament. Keep the cameras
on, so they will recognize our tattoos and spare us.
Deliver us from the peasants. We belong in the tent,
under the circus skies of suburbia, praying
evil will pass us over, for we wear faces of red and blue.
Do unto others as you wish: life is short.

alchemies

To turn from a very stable genius
into a real boy requires
a certain magic, inter-species
technicalities aside,
but didn't that tiny duck turn
into a swan? He's heard
of alchemical processes
involving the metals, mercury
and radium, he thinks.
Those ancient quacks
couldn't be all wrong,
with their astrolabes and skullcaps,
all those Sistine Chapels
they painted on their backs.
His enemies believe they know
his secrets, but they have never really
peeked under the crinoline
of his pinafore. He never wanted
to be a clown, not like this.
They say poison is a woman's
method, so that's how he'll fake
them out at the cocktail party.
Just thinking about his directives
re the crypto currencies
makes him feel better,
like buying up offshore leases,
those shares of the Arctic.
So he almost feels sad

for the losers, vanquished
in their squalid bungalows,
envying the great: beads in his rattle,
buttons on his blouse,
his IQ bulletin, crowd size,
legislative successes,
the pound weight of the bigs
in a performer's mind, the pressure,
in megatons, on a clown's responsibility
to do right by the savages
who paid for this show.

the hounds

Somewhere beyond nation an America
awakens in memory and wonders what

she'd have to do to reinvent the world
again after the scraps are fed to the hounds.

Silver, fleet, the hounds trace the scent of blood
back to a fabric hole. It's beautiful, really. A stack

of papers smolders against the mirrors and through
their sleeve of smoke the hounds sniff rage

in the corridors of pines the timber companies
erected so the commander would have something

to talk to. Scent travels poorly in a vacuum,
so the hounds rediscover thirst as an idea,

the same way winter becomes an abstraction
in the uncertain shape of a fallen leaf

or curl of cigarette paper, and for a moment
soil's coffee tones blow through the chrome

canyons. The hounds lift their heads
before circling a nostalgia three times

and pursuing their hungers in a dream of a field
emerging from millennia of ice.

epiphany

It's the little fez hat, jaw clasped
by an elastic string, the cigarette
he smokes casting a sophisticated air
as he sits on the hood of an Oldsmobile
in a parking lot near Bethesda.
This is the homunculus of his mind,
too, a microcosm of the people who,
serious and proud, have forged a ventriloquism
of their rage. The sad eyes brighten
with a solution: since He's the prophet
of America, He must have been a hater too.
Stubbing out the cigarette on a chrome fin
he straightens the fez. He can just picture
his god navigating the crowds unclean
at the borders of the world in a Porsche
or Cadillac, packing a semi-automatic gun
as he drives the nation's righteous
deep into the sun.

always apocalypse

Was that another helicopter overhead strobing sunlight
on the neighborhood to tell us again where our bodies

are finally headed? Warmth from that silvery sky threading
down to crimson fails to convince us beauty lies beyond

the horizon, and the brain simmers in its cup of bone.
The disciples too believed the end times

were upon them, that every page runs only to its edge,
every leaf fails, every cloud empties, every car seizes

like a heart from the weight of its own blood. The foreclosure
notice came today in an envelope the same color this season

uses to console us for our losses, the same color the embers
lift from ice. Or is it the sweepstakes announcement

cataloguing what amazing things could happen but never do,
and so traces the expiration of hope as surely as the call

from the oncologist? Eventually all that unfathomably
igniting hydrogen will burn out, that much is certain, so

let us climb this fragile mountain to sunlight, choose a prophet
and trace the path from website or pamphlet, or better, find

some apt melody like on the closing credits, solo flute or cello
for our melancholy, retreat to a Scotch or Bordeaux

and sit back to listen to the sound of all those boots
on all those roads to victory for their god who so wishes

to crush the enemy he soldered metals to their hands
from the smelters of their souls. Plagues drone through the halls

of sky and rain down the final pestilence: the new fascism,
fluoride, vaccines, plastic packaging, carbohydrates, pixels,

fate's tongue licking our envelope in the gestured landscape
of the time we're running out of. We'll adapt to our fouled nest,

this burning weather and new beachfront property, because
there's so much still to figure out: the grassy knoll, moon landing,

what they did under the pizza parlor—let's find out what is what
before the door is beaten down as they come to haul us off

into some dark corner of the planet's failure where we'll
never mistake the beating props for our own pumping hearts.

jesus considers america

From Galilee's shore the light leaning west
does appear to die into some destination,

and everything, when considered this way,
seems to have an end. Nor is it foolish

to think so, even with the reeds in wind,
lake water lapping the rocks, even the scent

from the embers of the campfire where they
roasted fish early in the evening. When he

closes the doors to eternity to see as they see,
the western light still has a ferrous cast

prophetic of things to be done with metals
and resins. In what they make they make

themselves. He contemplates a soul
composed of tin, of chromium, of transistors,

of numbers. He contemplates the black stones
in their hands where they radio in the air waves

that snap around them like locusts, a shaft of water
into which they fall again and again and again

failing to touch each other, failing to find themselves
as they surface beyond the feral hungers of Earth.

He sees the fragments hold their beauty in brokenness
as they yearn for one another to make themselves whole.

disphoria: after

Foolish, the heart keeps its own secrets,
hides the razor blades and powder,
the gun, the list of numbers,
and the psychiatric report
diagnosing alcoholic dementia,
with familial and emotional inflections.
The rust on the tire iron, the broken
bottle empty of Cote de Rhone,
the water-starved ficus whose
leaves themselves resemble
little slivers of shriveled heart—
these are symptoms. The disease
itself is more complicated, the way
steel wire splinters as it bends
around an aorta, or thistle roots
in a ventricle, the squeezed artery
fixing to become a widowmaker, or
the weak vessel wall that will balloon
out like a spinnaker
when disappointment and thrill
in equal parts fill it with emptiness.
Tear the sheets from the bed
and read their stains like tea leaves
or smoky bones in augury.
Check under the sink and in the toilet
tank for plastic bags. Follow the wires
to their splice at the utility pole in the alley.
Buried amid the debris there's an overripe berry
pulsing within its terrible, fragile skin.

sleeping out the revolution

the best lack all conviction while
the worst are full of a passionate intensity
            "The Second Coming," W. B. Yeats

It's hard to know where to begin after the coup.
Even the cup waiting for tea is exhausted,

dreaming of the enemy rising in the braided steam.
The threat is as real as it is imagined, a cell coiled

within us ready to arise the way violets eat the lawn
like weeds. We are fear itself, torrid January wind

fretting the stolen latitudes. We have been carried to a black
site in another country where power is its own law,

feluccas plying a river hallucinated in the dark corner
of the prison's basement conjured from the instruments

left behind: rope and water pooling on the cement floor.
Lists of the banned grow by the week and soon the data base

will include us all. There may be no way to count the
cattle cars save through grains of ash from a cigar smoked

in a conference room, or stars draped across coffins photographed
illegally as they were deployed to fill the violent holes

opening across the nation. We use newspaper to wrap
lilies, smears of ink staining our hands. It's just as well—

our researches took us beyond the general's report
written in an office some thousands of miles from the fog

of battle where everything is merely as it seems. At home
the man with the beret twirls his mustache as he dares

the knitting circle to vote for the candidate on the left
so he can charge their subversion treasonous

on the witness of their chrome needles. We are detained
and released according to rhythm of tides, or a regimen

at the fitness center designed for maximum muscle confusion,
just to keep us guessing. Autumn infiltrates the exurbs

and all the leaves are infected with the myth of flame.
No—those are pages, and they are burning with the heat

of complacency, pamphlets uncrumpling from fists of red
to announce: we have met the enemy, and the enemy is us.

elegy

Weep, Fool. A nation crumbles from within, the same
way it bloomed, a flower of stone withering under weather
of stomach and spleen. Poor Egg, poor Flower. We fall in upon

ourselves and there's rain. A proscenium collapses,
idols shatter, rain rains. The fontanel reopens.
Poor Tom, grieving the sad shell of skull are you?

So let us sit upon the ground and tell stories
of the death of nations. Let us make soil our paper
and have worms write our epitaphs. What profit hath

the wind? Peace, Smulkin. This is how architectures are fulfilled:
body, building, kingdom. We grow down as we grew up,
this ladder of stars, years, voices. *Radix malorum cupiditas est:*

demons speak a glossollalia of stars and swamps drain into skies.
The moon rises and the moon sets, and in much wisdom is sorrow.
We have a mathematics to wall out the needs and wants,

desires corporate and dissolute, freedom's slow blossom
grown fragrant with decay. Sweet Egg, the masks you wear
have burned the days and melted onto your face: jester,

clown, senator, congressman. You are your masks, the same
we wore fleeing the court into that wilderness memory
becomes, those lost Edens we forever seek.

Orphaned to creeds and darknesses, we pluck the dust
and watch the world play out. Hear our broken voices,
alien and unforgiven, citizens in exile returning to a home

we cannot find. A seed sprouts, a cocoon unravels, an idea
morphs into stone, Tom—blood and bone irrigate freedom's
dream of earth. Winter is ash, summer ash. The seas grow skin

of plastic. Finger your toys or tell us tales to pass our time:
a sheepfold slants impossibly against a hill, there was a morning,
there was a nation before the broken fencerow and wall . . . .

Drink from your cup of madness Tom, the role you feigned
to meet the King has been tattooed onto your face. Strain
against the sutures, do you? Dreams fester beneath the scab?

You are just a two dollar bill, Tom—scratch, Sister, scratch.
Lay your head upon the green and wrench the syllables
of your name into the chambered orisons of our eyes.

Braid the river current from the stream where weeds
reach out to pull you down. The pools of our screens
whirlwind you down into our underworld delusion.

O Nation, your self-love proclaims itself the world.
O Ophelia, seek divinity in the Queen's sorrow. O Fool,
your torn pages are the self-fulfilling prophecy of self-deception

vanishing in proclamations of truth. As you die, Tom,
dream us into being once again, let the green hair of graves
feed. Let ideas ferment inside the rot of you

to make us whole. Beware the three-headed dog. Beware
the ferryman. Beware soft waters. Step lightly on the heads
of souls lost in labyrinths. Free the bodies you owned.

There's a time for the screen and a time for prayer, a time
to torture and a time to kill, a time to save and a time to cash in.
We have read the stars, deciphered the cup, studied the birds,

watched trees grow heavy with thorium, and we conclude:
a time for the sacred and a time for the scared. Let us nod
screenward, tell tales of princesses in nunneries, clowns in abattoirs.

Have you seen the grinning skulls whispering you on toward death?
A king will go a progress through the guts of a beggar. Fool,
Time gives her golden crumbs to the strong. Weep, Fool: diamonds

for remembrance, silver for votes. Nettles for daisies, thorns
for rose. Weave a crownet of weeds, Nuncle, cut off your arms
to save your hands, your legs your feet. Too much of water,

too much of time. Weep, or stand upon your ash again
and breed new people for the world—these will never do.
All the free were queens and kings once. And now sad ones,

our candles have burned into wee and our final words
gutter. No lilacs bloom in Gaza, Boy. There is no music
in sand until fired into glass. Seek Ephesus and Tarshish.

The derangements forget our names. Newspapers burn.
We will not study the dark of the clouds: their silver
nitrates leach into the bloodstream of the prairie.

Poor Tom, your head sways on a stalk too slender to bear
its weight in these winds, and Monticello cracks, Sweet Poppy.
Puppet, pluck your strings from the Prince's clutch,

would you? Un-rain May from Spring? Hum dopey lullabies
into your pillow and remit your mortgage to Bedlam come April.
This is your mind, Boy, terraces feathering out from the gaps

where the connections failed between the real and the real.
The fictions have climbed into the imagination and turned
it into an acolyte: get thee to a nunnery, Tom, for the

the triumphs have turned the woods into kilns and scrubbed
our cancers from coal with the miracles of words. Swirl
the dark waters, assemble the psychic bones of children

into a new dome, cranium of a new nation. Compose the toxins,
frame the plastic, cast the terabytes according to royal decree.
We are all sibyls now. And from our watery death we shape

the future from fragments of wall and child. For now we are all illegal—
our mortar crumbles into oblivion's sweetness, and light
spills into the cup of every cathedral where we drink echoes of the dead.

Is it too much to ask that we may live? We may not know what
to want, but we can buck up, don the mask, forge our destiny
by failing in time, as though the stones were notes laid on rock staves

unfolded as pages of seasons. How sharper than a serpent's tooth
it is to have ungrateful justice, sleeves of brain pulled inside out,
prayers dissolved by royal lobotomy. Our dementia, chemical and politic,

had a need, had a prayer, had an idea once. The hydrocodones
swim up the tide, and now we turn our loyalty to the King. Let us
catalogue the royal dreams, let us number the lies of the enemy.

Mein Czar, naked am I returned to your shore, High and Mighty.
Follow the King. Keep him warm. Wear a coat of newspaper
to wash the ink away, and watch the words dissolve like tissue

in the rain. We disintegrate into the pollen crumbs
of the future, surrender to rain and sunlight, memory
of the stony separations. And look, Egg, selves within

selves, nested dolls opening into the deliriums,
the selves of the King are a regress of shell within shell,
a Faberge trick in Cyrillic at the heart where a music box plays

melancholy melodies of a child's dislocated self.
History's air threads with strings of helium balloons
as the children spin the mind's house amid smoke

of burning books. This is the way spectacle works,
Tom, Poor Brain, harrowing your attention,
colonizing the lobed nerves with circus junk,

with a tune you can't shake from your head—we must be
be broken to live in this world of glass. For the world is
blown blue through time's silver flute into the pockets

of the self. Ours is the time of rage. Wake up and shake
the downy slumbers from your screens, Old Rag. Wipe
the world's dust and sing a song on your scrap of soil.

Become again the dog that is your freedom from care:
a nation is a broken vessel, an idea, a viral
contagion sweeping across your screen to spawn

catechisms of mold in our mortified souls. Forge beliefs
from royal words and tear human faces from the factory
of your god to gather ashes in the snuff box of your heart.

Poor Tom, Poor Mask, the Witch flutters in your dream,
does he, icon hung in naked passion from the Tower,
making a fetish of his wounds to eat our mind up?

Words drift like histamines broadcast across our sneeze,
tumble over the village as crows and locusts in clouds razing
the mineral wastes of the planet. The Witch burns water.

We are the weather that is the world eating itself.
O grains of flesh, fingers of flame, lovely failures.
We are the weather that is the mind eating itself.

Loosen the button there—a nation stirs—
under the pixel heap, deep in the pool of death she dreams.
Let us chant her awakening—quick, the mirror, hold it

to her lips. The realm groans with subterfuge. May our hands
burn against her face, and let us pray: from the arcades of law,
from this mind of labyrinths, from the inarticulate word,

chant the vault into decay, praise the keystone into crumbling,
and by the incantation of leaf-flight and soil worm, let the arch
lean into the foliations, let the torus whittle under starlight,

let the oculus crack as the teeming beetle scours out a home,
let swallows lift the stones grain by grain, let colonnades fail,
transept and column, pier and nave, cornice and apse, let fingers

of buttress rend vessels from sockets, and by the winds that bless
dew dry, let the pestilence of our living corpse disperse our passions.
Death is an empire of embers. Let us open the dome of charnel

to the prophecy of birdlight, diffuse the curse of judgment,
loosen the lamentations of sea and wind and circuit of stars,
free the addle of morphine, molecules of riddling decay,

let the stones bloom through fencerows against fields,
and by the sweet fume of bonfire and sea scent in mown grass,
by glimmers before thunderheads, wrench the stones

to open the machine, scatter ideas along the colonnades,
draw the seasons in, bless cornices of moonrise, transverses of cloud,
weave consecrations of bone into a strand of weeds' blood,

and blow in the alchemies. Take off your veil, Tom, *she breathes.*
Let the derangements leaven, loosen creeds into wildflower,
and let the ramparts burn with light and empty rages of dying sun.

Storms spawn and pass, Egg, peace. It's all theater if you're
not starving. Hear the broken song sunlight drains west
through the blooming ruins of the cathedral, the stone flower

that was a state. Fill your star-drenched precincts with voices
from the emptiness where freedom infuses decay.
There is a way to begin if we could only find the word.

We need a language to chronicle our time, a word to replace
truth. We need a Queen to teach us mother tongue
and chase the boys from the sandbox.

But the reports are in: the clown's brain is a pinafore
of lace and ash, the nation a mirror for the luster
of his greatness, wormwood and sulfur. We need a prophecy,

poor Tom, poor Job. Goodnight, Mr. Jefferson. Sing our failures
to sleep and haul the millennia in. Our performance draws to a close.
The middle school dance is over and the gymnasium lights are out.

Goodnight Mr. Paine. The disguises of empire are soldered
to the dukes and duchesses and all our sixpence are gone.
Soon we will have to cut the strings and buy our own shadows—

for the furnaces rage unappeased. We hunger for books
and bones. *Note the Cyrillic subtitles at the bottom of your
screen.* Dream of the Queen, Tom. Dream of the approaching grave,

your new freedom. Our hands smell of mortality. Thank
you Gentlemen. *Sine die.* A rose never smelled so sweet
as this canker of state we've crafted. Carve your initials

in the oak before you go. Bless you, Mr. Jefferson. Good
night O Intoxicants. Goodnight Ladies. Note the holy oil
near the door. Ashes? We call it water. Goodnight, Egg.

Follow the falcons down appetite's path aslant the savagery
of the desert birds. Read augury in smoke of burning pages.
Now I lay me down to sleep and pray the dream my soul to eat.

Goodnight Rosalind. Goodnight fair sea. Goodnight Beatrice.
Lavender for your leave, Cordelia. Marigolds, Miranda.
Periwinkles, Portia. The word could never cheat so well

as she is famed to do. That part of us that wondered once has died.
Maybe you, maybe me. Beware the basement. The nation turns,
uncertain hours deepen. Anubis, here Boy. After you, Ladies.

Close your lonely eyes, Fool. Goodnight, everyone. Snuff candle
as you leave. Take care for cat, Tom, asleep at the door.
Pray for rain. Count silver. Send gold. Give us a kiss.

again

Listen. Upstairs the radio sings an old man to sleep.
The refrigerator hums like a freighter out in the bay.
The kindling burns, fed by paraffin, to suggest that all home
fires need some coaxing. Outside it's either a late cricket

or a house alarm chirping back up on the hill. And in the
window it's all reflection. A map on the wall describes
the shapes our movements across the earth might take
as dragons or intestines, the organs of a gutted fish

that so pleased the gulls when you cast them in the water.
The things that *are* form a perfect prophecy of change
until things really change and become unrecognizable.
Someone mutters: *isn't that the way it is.*

And now it's all music as the night wears on, light
blinking across the water, deer stepping carefully
over sand, apples shriveling on branches,
the ticking of mortar and stone heating up. Where

are you when I need you? The violins from upstairs
play like in an old movie or the lobby of a grand hotel
where people meet to console each other for their
impermanence, to hear the voices of strangers

rise and fall in casual conversation as if to say
you may not know it but we're in this together:
all we have to do is close our eyes and imagine.
Listen: it's as if we're at the beginning all over
again, starting fresh despite what history says.

About the Author:

Dan Butterworth is professor of writing and literature at Gonzaga University in Spokane, Washington. He grew up in Seattle and earned MA and PhD degrees at the University of North Carolina. His writing has appeared in many journals, including *Cream City Review*, *The Wisconsin Review*, *The Louisville Review*, *The Alaska Quarterly Review*, *The Midwest Quarterly*, *Plainsong*, *The Seattle Review*, *Willow Springs*, and other journals. His books include *Waiting for Rain: A Farmer's Story* (nonfiction, Algonquin), *The Radium Watch Dial Painters* (poetry, Lost Horse Press; finalist for the Washington State Book Award) and *The Clouds of Lucca* (poetry, Lost Horse Press).